GUN CONTROL

GUN
CONTROL

Renardo Barden

The Rourke Corporation, Inc.

The Rourke Corporation, Inc.
P.O. Box 3328, Vero Beach, FL 32964

Barden, Renardo.
    Gun control / by Renardo Barden.
       p. cm. — (Troubled society)
    Includes bibliographical references (p. 63) and index.
    Summary: Presents both sides of the gun control debate while describing some of the more shocking incidents in which the use of guns played a tragic role.
    ISBN 0-86593-072-4
    1. Gun Control—United States—Juvenile literature. [1. Gun control.] I. Title. II. Series.
HV7436.B37   1990
363.3'3'0973—dc20   90-8783
                                                    CIP
                                                      AC

Series Editor: Gregory Lee
Editors: Elizabeth Sirimarco, Marguerite Aronowitz
Book design and production: The Creative Spark,
    Capistrano Beach, CA
Cover photograph: David M. Doody/Tom Stack & Associates

GUN CONTROL

Contents

ONE

BAD DAYS IN AMERICA

On January 17, 1989, a 24-year-old welder named Patrick Edward Purdy parked his old station wagon near Cleveland Elementary School in Stockton, California, where he had attended school as a boy.

He carried an AK-47 assault rifle and a Taurus 9 millimeter semiautomatic pistol with him as he walked toward the playground where about 400 children were playing. Without warning, he opened fire with the rifle. Within moments Purdy fired more than 100 shots from his $350 weapon. Tragically, many of Purdy's bullets found targets. Thirty-five people were struck: 29 school children and one teacher. Five children between the ages of six and nine were killed.

Although assault weapons were designed for modern warfare, they are readily available for sale in gun shops all across America. Assault rifles enable the user to fire as many as 75 rounds (bullets) very quickly and without reloading. Anyone over 21 can buy one, even people with mental problems like Purdy.

After shooting down the school children with his AK-47, Purdy fired the smaller weapon. He shot himself in the head and died. There was no explanation for this senseless killing.

The murdered and wounded children were of Cambodian descent. Their families came from the war-ravaged Southeast Asian country of Cambodia, near Vietnam. Purdy's father had been discharged from the army for mental problems after having served in Vietnam. Perhaps Purdy learned to hate people from Southeast Asia because of his mentally disturbed father. We will never know.

The happy sounds of a school playground were turned into cries of terror when a
man with a rifle shot and killed six children and wounded many others
in Stockton, California, in 1989.

Purdy's schoolyard massacre outraged
Americans from coast to coast. And it raised once
again a continuing debate in American life—the issue
of gun control.

Buying Guns

Because firearms are so portable and easy to
take from one city or state to another, they are very
difficult to regulate (that means to control through
laws). For example, Purdy lived in California, but he
legally bought his AK-47 in an Oregon gunshop and

legally transported it to California in his car. Criminals and killers often buy their weapons in states where laws controlling gun sales and use are virtually nonexistent. And gun laws differ from state to state or county to county.

For example, in some states, a man or woman wanting to buy a gun must fill out an application and be investigated by local authorities before they are allowed to take the weapon home. This waiting period might be for three, seven, 15 or 30 days. Other states have no waiting period, so a buyer can always travel to another state to buy a gun.

States such as New York and Massachusetts require gun buyers to wait several days or even weeks before they can claim their weapons. But in Texas, Virginia, Georgia and some other states, guns can be bought with cash, "no questions asked." In fact, some people make a living buying guns in states like Texas and Georgia then taking them to areas with more restrictive laws where they can sell them at a high profit. A semiautomatic handgun that sells for $300 in Florida, for example, can be resold for $1,000 in New York. People who do this are called "gun runners," and gun running can be nearly as profitable as drug dealing.

Consider this muddled situation. Multnomah County, which includes part of the city of Portland, Oregon, recently passed a law restricting the use and transportation of assault weapons in Multnomah County. But since the city of Portland is only partly situated in Multnomah County, the law doesn't apply to the whole city. Portland is also just a ten-minute drive from Vancouver, Washington, where assault weapons are still legal. Although the Multnomah County law may make it easier for police to arrest someone misusing a gun in the restricted section of Portland, the law is not likely to have much impact on the number of shootings that occur in either the city or the state.

Because of confusing local laws like these, any realistic discussion of gun "control" must be treated on a national basis.

The United States today is a country flooded with guns. Authorities estimate that as many as 75 million firearms are owned by 50 million American households. With this many guns around, it is not surprising that thousands of Americans lose their lives to gunshot wounds each year.

Many of those who die as a result of gunfire are young and innocent, and many who kill are also young and naive about gun use. Some killers are so young they do not grasp the finality of death. Some probably do not really understand the difference between a make-believe television death where an actor gets up and walks away, and a real gunshot death, where a human life is gone forever.

The Story Of Juan And Jacalyn

On December 18, 1989, Juan Cardenas went to pick up his girlfriend, Jacalyn Calabrese, from her home. The two seventh graders had planned a trip to a shopping mall in suburban Los Angeles. At the mall, they met up with other friends. Twelve-year-old Juan had a crush on Jacalyn and wanted her to admire him. But she was hard to impress.

For several weeks he had been carrying a small, semi-automatic pistol. At the mall he began showing it off, waving the .25-caliber gun in the air and taking aim at his friends. Clowning around and having what he thought of as fun, Juan pointed the pistol at another classmate, 12-year-old Keli Edwards. Keli swore at him and ran away in fear.

But Jacalyn Calabrese did not believe the gun was real. She was like Juan and liked to act tough. She teased him, saying the gun wasn't real.

"Come on, Juan, shoot me," Jacalyn dared him.

Juan thought he would scare Jacalyn. Quickly, he removed the bullet from the pistol's chamber and aimed the handgun at her forehead. He did not know that this pistol automatically chambers (loads) another bullet. Jacalyn stepped back a few paces and continued to tease him. Juan steadied the pistol with two hands and pulled the trigger. To his surprise, the pistol discharged.

Jacalyn put her hands to her forehead and fell down, bloodying the tiled floor of the mall.

In a panic, Juan ran. Witnesses said he was yelling, "Oh my God! Oh my God!" Two security guards chased him, but were unable to catch him.

Some shoppers heard the gunfire and ducked into stores. Others waited until Juan ran out, then rushed to see if they could do something to help. Some tried to stop the blood flowing from the hole in Jacalyn's head.

One of Jacalyn's friends ran to call Jacalyn's parents. Her 15-year-old sister Angie and mother Gloria rushed to the mall as fast as they could.

"I pushed my way through the crowd and I remember seeing a big pool of blood," said Angie. Jacalyn's body lay on the tile floor between some pot-

The Stockton schoolyard massacre ended when Patrick Purdy, the
man who calmly fired a semiautomatic weapon at a playground full of children,
took his own life.

ted plants. Angie never even got to say goodby to her
sister. Jacalyn Calabrese was dead.

   With a helicopter and dogs, police searched the
nearby neighborhood for Juan, who had run to a
friend's house about half a mile from the shopping cen-
ter. "Help me, Mike," Juan said to his friend, "I think I've

killed someone."

Mike's father said Juan appeared to be very afraid and cried a lot during the next two hours. Finally, he told Juan he should call his mother. Juan's mother arrived shortly afterwards with police officers, who took Juan into custody.

The next day at Cerro Villa Middle School, where Jacalyn and Juan had attended seventh grade, the American flag flew at half-mast. Nine psychologists were at the school to talk to students about understanding and accepting Jacalyn's death. But no one could explain why Juan had done what he did.

"They wonder how could this possibly happen to a friend," one of the psychologists said. "They want to blame somebody so the whole incident can be resolved immediately. Some side with Jackie, some side with the boy."

In trying to understand why a 12-year-old boy would be carrying a pistol, police questioned those who knew him. Two classmates said he carried the weapon because he wanted to impress a local gang called the Highland Street Crips.

Because Jacalyn died, some people thought Juan should be tried for manslaughter, a very serious criminal charge. Others thought the shooting was accidental and that Juan should not be charged with committing any crime.

The authorities decided to bring charges of involuntary manslaughter against Juan. In their view, he had been criminally negligent in playing with a gun he knew was loaded. By "negligence" the prosecuting lawyers meant that in their opinion, Juan had failed to use a reasonable amount of care in handling the pistol.

Juan was found guilty. Moments before he was sentenced, Jacalyn's mother confronted the boy. "Juan, I would like to know why you shot my daughter," said Gloria Calabrese. "I would like to know what you think you deserve for punishment. My daughter didn't deserve this."

Juan did not have an answer.

Juan was sentenced to spend one year in Juvenile Hall. Upon hearing the sentence, both Jacalyn's and Juan's parents were in tears. The boy's father, Juan Cardenas, Sr., told the judge that he and not the boy should be imprisoned, "because if I had not permitted this firearm to be brought in my house, none of this would ever have happened." He explained that his son found the gun hidden under some old clothes in the garage. Without the knowledge of his parents, he began carrying it to impress and frighten his friends.

Juan's attorney summed up the tragedy: "There's no way the girl can be brought back. There's no way the family of the girl can have solace [comfort]. There's no way the family of Juan can ever be what it was before. There's no way Juan can ever forget this."

A Terrible Trend

David Abrecht, a police captain in Garden Grove, California, found the shooting of Jacalyn Calabrese to be doubly disturbing. Apart from the tragedy involving the two families, Abrecht believes that the shooting is part of a trend. "We are definitely seeing an increase in the number of kids with guns," he said.

Abrecht should know. Three months before Juan shot Jacalyn, two people were killed and six others wounded in the small city of Garden Grove. Police later arrested a 14-year-old alleged gang member and charged him with the killings.

Less than one month later, a 15-year-old boy who lived near Disneyland in Anaheim, California, walked into his drama class and shot a classmate in the face. Then he held the other students hostage for more than 30 minutes. The guns the boy used belonged to his parents.

Many young people are the innocent victims of gunshots—as they were when Patrick Purdy shot up the Stockton schoolyard. Sometimes—as was the case with Juan and Jacalyn—they are killed by accident because the shooter fails to realize that just one mistake with a gun can mean instant death for an innocent victim. A young person can also get a gun and, in a moment of panic, endanger not only his or her own life but the lives of others—not in hatred, but in terror.

The Death Of Timothy Baumel

An example of this happened on Friday, November 27, 1987, after 14-year-old Timothy Baumel returned home from Christmas shopping in Portland, Oregon. He was having a bad day. He had a temper tantrum and tore down "for sale" signs in front of the house. He kicked the car. Then he and his mother had a fight. In his rage, the boy got a .22-caliber rifle from his room and threatened his family. His 17-year-old brother Kenny and 12-year-old sister Jane hid in the garage. His mother called the police and told them that her son was armed and out of control.

Full of anger and fear, Timothy Baumel left his house, gun in hand. He ran for 15 blocks, cutting through yards, frightening and endangering neighbors. The police arrived and gave chase. When police closed in on Timothy, he aimed at them and fired twice. The police fired back, killing him with two blasts from a shotgun. They did not want to shoot him, but they were afraid for their own lives.

The death of Timothy Baumel is especially disturbing because he died as a result of not being able to control his emotions. It is disturbing to think that someone should die because of a moment of intense anger and fear. The police who killed Timothy were very upset afterward, but their gunshots could not be taken back.

The Gun Culture

Unfortunately for today's society, these shootings are not isolated events. They are part of a larger shadow of gun death in the United States. Although violence from guns is nothing new, gunshot victims keep getting younger and younger. In fact, gunshot wounds have become the fourth leading cause of death among people under 14 years of age, says Nancy Gannon, assistant director of Handgun Control, Inc., a national organization that works for gun control laws.

Many of these deaths are not homicides, but rather suicides. Every day, somewhere in the United States, a handgun is lifted out of a drawer and starts a family nightmare. Weighed down by moods of depression and hopelessness, many teenagers kill themselves with their parents' handguns. One suicide authority, aware that unhappy moods come and go in the lives of the young, calls suicide "a permanent solution to a temporary problem."

American cities are flooded with unregistered handguns; that is, if the gun is used in the commission of a crime, it is difficult to trace the owner. As many as 100,000 guns are stolen from homes and businesses each year by drug dealers and gang members who use them to commit crimes, then give or sell them to other criminals.

But guns are not only a problem with young people who kill themselves or deal drugs. Deaths caused by guns are a national epidemic—like a disease—that claim the lives of thousands of Americans of all ages every year.

In a land where authorities estimate that there is one gun for every four people, a gun is sometimes easier to find than a helping hand, or even a telephone.

Guns are a part of the American culture, and always have been—from the days of the American revolution and Davey Crockett to movie heroes like "Rambo." Guns are specifically mentioned in our Constitution. The Second Amendment gives every American the "right to bear arms," and this right is staunchly defended by gun owners who fear that any attempt by government to control gun ownership is a direct attack on their civil rights. When people try to pass laws to control gun ownership and use, they are consistently met with strenuous opposition by many gun owners.

Those who want some kind of gun control (called gun control proponents) do not believe the Second Amendment should prevent government from passing laws to restrict what kinds of guns should be legal, and what they can be used for. Both sides of this debate are convinced they are right and the other side is wrong. In the following chapters we will explore some of the issues from both sides.

TWO

A Bloody Issue

Partly as a response to the horror most people felt after the Stockton school massacre, *Time* magazine decided to record all gunshot deaths that occurred in the United States during just one week. The staff writers chose the first week of May 1989—a "normal" week. During those seven days, 464 people died of gunshot wounds.

Time then published a story about the victims entitled "7 Deadly Days" in its July 17 issue. Editors searched for and reproduced photos of the victims. Each photo was accompanied by information about the circumstances of the victim's death. They were of all ages and races. Some lived in cities and some in rural communities. They came from 42 of the 50 states. The youngest was only two years old, while the oldest was 87. African-Americans, whites, Asians and Hispanics made up the list of victims. Death was colorblind.

During the years 1984 and 1985, 62,897 people in the United States died from gunshot injuries. These are more people than were killed during the Vietnam War, which lasted more than eight years. Based on these numbers and on the sample week's toll, *Time* editors predicted that close to 30,000 people in America would die of gunshot wounds in 1989.

Surprisingly, many Americans are not shocked by this continuing national tragedy. In fact, many believe all these deaths are an unfortunate but necessary price to pay for American freedom under the Second Amendment.

Violence At Home And Abroad

For many years, hundreds of thousands of Americans called loudly for the Vietnam War to be

Edward D. Conroy of the Bureau of Alcohol, Tobacco and Firearms holds up an assault rifle while testifying before a Senate subcommittee about semiautomatic weapons and their use. The importation of semiautomatic weapons was banned in 1989 by Congress.

brought to an end. The war eventually cost more than 50,000 American lives. And yet, few Americans have ever protested the toll of Americans killed by domestic gunfire. In 1988 and 1989 alone, more people were killed by gunshots than have yet died of AIDS. Few are making a widespread effort to reduce the number of gun deaths.

Deaths caused by car accidents each year exceed the number of shooting deaths, but cars are constantly inspected for safety. In most states, wearing seatbelts is required by law. Drivers are routinely examined to make sure they know the driving laws and have adequate vision. Drunk drivers, who cause many serious accidents, can be fined, put in jail, and have their driver's licenses taken away. Automobile safety is big business in the United States, but scarcely any money at all is spent to protect potential victims from being shot by a gun.

Why do so many people buy and own guns? Many people say they want to be able to defend themselves and their loved ones from violent intruders. The *Time* story, however, reported that deaths involving self-defense were rare. In fact, only 14 out of the 464 deaths involved self-defense. Police believe that if a household gun is used at all, it is six times more likely to be fired at a member of the family who owns it or at a friend than at an intruder. More likely still is that the gun will be stolen. Burglars always search out and take guns, knowing they can be used or resold to other criminals.

Of the 464 gun-related deaths during that week in 1989, only a little more than half were murders. The other half were suicides. Angry, depressed, or in ill health, 216 people shot themselves to death. Of the 216, nine killed someone else first—usually spouses, lovers or relatives. Twenty-two deaths (five percent) were accidents, eight more than those resulting from guns fired in self-defense. About 15 percent (66) of the gunshot victims were under age 21. *Time* magazine concluded that "guns most often kill the people who own them or people whom the owners know well."

America is the most gun-loving nation in the world. If we add the populations of Japan, Canada

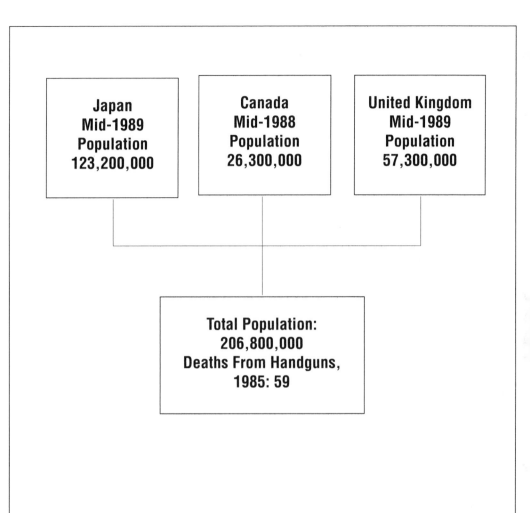

Japan
Mid-1989
Population
123,200,000

Canada
Mid-1988
Population
26,300,000

United Kingdom
Mid-1989
Population
57,300,000

Total Population:
206,800,000
Deaths From Handguns,
1985: 59

United States Mid-1989
Population
248,800,000
Deaths From Handguns,
1985: 8,092

Source: *The 1990 Almanac*. Houghton Mifflin Company, Boston, 1990

and Great Britain, we would have a total population nearly equal in size to that of the United States. Yet in 1985, only 59 people were killed with handguns in those three countries combined. That same year in the United States, 8,092 were killed by handguns.

Notice that the number 8,092 is a lot smaller than the 30,000 that Time predicted would be killed in 1989. The reason is that the 30,000 figure was based on all gun deaths—whether by shotgun, handgun, rifle, or assault rifle. The 8,092 deaths were by handgun alone.

Statistics can sometimes be confusing, and often they seem to contradict other statistics and polls. It is necessary to read and compare numbers closely. For example, the Department of Justice says that more than 27,000 young people between the ages of 12 and 15 were victims of handgun violence in 1985. Again, this represents handguns only. The 27,000 victims included young people who were shot and killed, robbed, threatened, shot at and missed, and those injured while trying to get away from somebody who was aiming a gun at them. Twenty-seven thousand people are as many as the entire population of Grand Junction, Colorado.

Guns: An American Tradition

When the first settlers began arriving in the New World from Spain, England and France, guns were essential to the methods those countries used when colonizing new territories such as North and South America.

In Mexico and South America, the Spanish conquistadors and clergy sought to convert the natives to the Catholic faith. In the process they helped them-selves to the Indians' gold, food, and whatever else they wanted. They made war on those who refused to cooperate. Without the gun and the sword, Spain could not have conquered the Native Americans and secured a role for itself in the Americas.

The British and the French settled primarily in North America, where the natives had little gold and few treasures. But they had one thing the British and the French wanted: land. The white colonists out-gunned the Native Americans for a great while, although Indians eventually obtained guns and learned to use them, holding their own in full-fledged warfare.

America was also full of wild game. Most colonists used guns to kill birds and other animals for fresh meat. Fur trappers hunted with guns, and to pro-tect themselves against bear, cougar and wolf. Men defended their mining claims with guns. Guns were often the only law in the new American wilderness, and guns were carried for protection against thieves.

Guns also enabled the first white settlers and trappers to insist on the white man's way of doing things. African slaves in the southern United States and the islands of the Caribbean were kept from revolting against their white masters by the gun.

Guns And Independence

Of course guns were essential to American inde-pendence. When many of the New England settlers began asserting themselves against their "mother country," England, large numbers of people who lived in the original 13 colonies rose up to be independent—

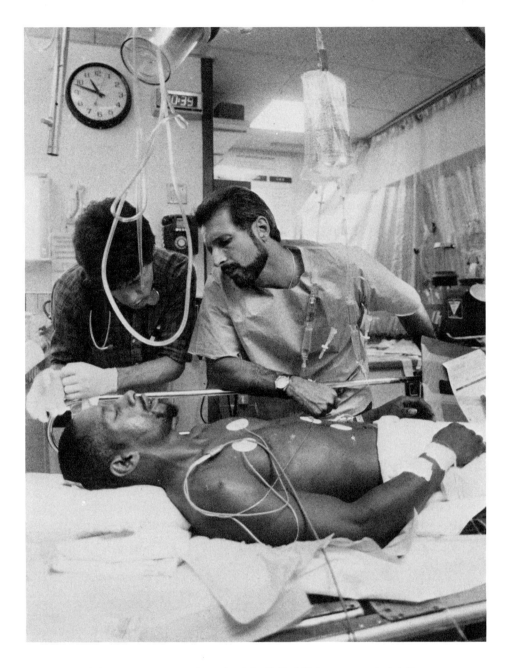

Hospital emergency rooms throughout the United States see gunshot victims every day. Hundreds of Americans are shot and killed each week. Many shootings are accidental, some are suicides, and many more are crime-related.

free of English laws and restrictions. When King George refused to grant the colonies more participation in decisions that affected them, the colonists rebelled. The result was the War for Independence (1775-1783).

The original 13 colonies had their own approaches to government. They were different from one another and often did not agree with the other colonies. Thinking men, however, realized that if the colonies were to achieve independence from England, they would have to learn to get along with one another. They also saw that it would be necessary to form a national government to help organize and regulate state governments. A federal government was formed that could, when necessary, tell the various states what to do. But the states did not want to give up all their individual freedoms, so they insisted that the new federal government be a limited one.

The Second Amendment

The United States Constitution was written to define the way that federal or national government would work. It was a document jointly written by the new states to keep them out of conflict with one another. In fact, most early Americans were nearly as afraid of the power of the federal government as they had been of the power of England and France.

Many people were dissatisfied with the Constitution. They wanted guarantees that the federal government would not attempt to take away their hard-won American freedoms. The result was the Bill of Rights, the first ten amendments to the Constitution. These amendments promised, among other things, the freedoms of religion, speech, and assembly.

The Second Amendment concerned the rights of individual states to maintain their own armies or militias, and the rights of the people living in those states to keep and bear arms. This right to have small state armies was considered very important by the writers of the Constitution. Democracy could survive, they reasoned, only as long as citizens retained control of the weapons they would need in order to fight for liberty and stand up against tyrants. At that time in history, most governments only allowed soldiers to have guns. The Second Amendment reversed this historic trend.

Although it is brief, the Second Amendment has been the subject of many disputes, and still is. Scholars have analyzed it and interpreted it differently. This is what it says, in its entirety:

"A well-regulated militia being necessary to the security of a free state, the right of the people to keep and bear arms shall not be infringed."

These seem to be straightforward words, but some things are not always what they seem. Some people argue that the most important part of this amendment is the right of a state to have a "well-regulated militia." Every state in the late 1700s considered it essential to maintain its own defense force, and that the right to bear arms was only for the convenience of raising a civilian militia in times of emergency. This era, of course, has long faded in the realities of the 20th century, where threats to America's borders are unlikely.

Others insist that the primary purpose of the amendment is stated clearly: "the right of the people to keep and bear arms shall not be infringed." The result? Government cannot tyrannize the people as long as the people are capable of fighting back. Gun control opponents see this as an unvarnished fact, with obvious relevance to all our other freedoms.

Many of today's Americans who believe in some form of gun control argue that the right to bear arms can be restricted by society if it will increase public safety. Put simply, many Americans do not want to guarantee this right to everyone who drives by a gun shop with enough cash.

Gun control opponents, on the other hand, argue that if the writers of the Constitution meant only for a militia to have the arms, they would have said "soldiers" rather than "the people."

Published accounts of the men who wrote and approved the Second Amendment, however, do not include any debate whatsoever about an individual's right to bear arms. Debate seems to have focused on the right of a state to keep a militia and defend itself against its enemies. So what would the founding fathers say about today's debate? We can only guess.

THREE

GUNS AND POLITICS

The axe was important to early settlers for building homes and clearing land for roads. The plow was important because it enabled men to prepare the ground for planting. The railroad and steamboat moved freight and people from one end of the country to the other. But for shaping our way of life, guns may be the single most important device used to write American history.

What would our society today be like if there had been fewer guns? What if some of our most important leaders had not been assassinated in recent times? Because many people have asked these questions, many more Americans now question the intentions of the men who wrote the Second Amendment.

America's Many Losses

John F. Kennedy was elected president in 1960. He became president at a time when America felt good about itself and its role in the world. Yet Americans and peoples of the world lived in fear of nuclear war. Kennedy urged young Americans to set aside purely materialistic goals and work for the betterment of all mankind. He put words into action by founding the Peace Corps, an organization of volunteers who traveled to other countries to teach people needed skills and improve the quality of their lives. When Kennedy was killed by gunfire on November 22, 1963, part of America stopped believing it could change the world for the better. Many Americans despaired of the future.

By preaching peace and love, American civil rights movement leader Martin Luther King, Jr., inspired millions

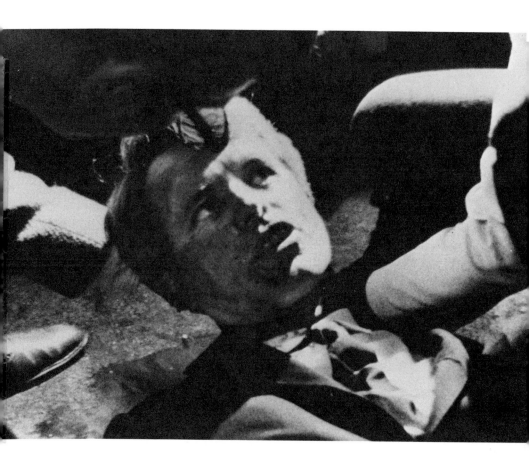

Senator Robert Kennedy lies mortally wounded in a Los Angeles hotel corridor after being shot by a man with a handgun. Kennedy had just won the 1968 California Democratic primary in his bid to become president.

of people of all races to support the cause of racial equality. In April 1968, King was shot and killed in Memphis, Tennessee. Millions of Americans, but particularly African-Americans, were enraged. It seemed to many that leaders who spoke of building a better America were always assassinated. Many African-Americans said that King's death proved he had been wrong about his philosophy of nonviolence. They began to believe that only by meeting violence with violence could racial equality be achieved. Grief and anger led to rioting in American city streets, and a worsening of racial tensions between whites and blacks.

John Kennedy's brother Bobby supported the civil rights movement, and believed that America should not fight the Vietnam War. He became a presidential candidate in 1968 and promised to end the war and work for racial equality. But only two months after Dr. King was killed, Kennedy was shot to death in Los Angeles. He never had the chance to bring the troops home from Vietnam.

When Kennedy and King were killed within months of each other, the nation was angry and bewildered. Newspapers, magazines and television stations studied the lives of the men who had gunned down these important men.

Reporters wrote stories about the guns used in the assassinations, and where and how the killers had acquired their weapons. For instance, John Kennedy's alleged assassin, Lee Harvey Oswald, bought his rifle through the mail from an advertisement in a rifle magazine. Sirhan B. Sirhan killed Bobby Kennedy with a cheap .22-caliber pistol. Sirhan's weapon was small and easy to hide. Similar weapons had often been used in weekend crime sprees and impulse murders. For that reason, such guns were nicknamed "Saturday night specials." For the first time, Americans awakened to the fact of how easily and cheaply anyone could acquire a rifle or weapon and use it to kill people.

The Birth Of Gun Control
In response to the Kennedy and King assassina-

Small, inexpensive handguns that are easily concealed are a favorite of robbers. They earned the nickname "Saturday night specials" because of their frequent use during weekend crimes throughout America.

tions, Congress decided that it should be made more difficult for Americans to obtain inexpensive guns. Although many objected, Congress passed the Gun Control Act of 1968.

Many hunters and target shooters were very angry with the new law. They claimed it placed a hardship on hunters and responsible gun owners. They warned that the law violated the Second Amendment, and insisted that the Gun Control Act interfered with "the right to bear arms."

The Gun Control Act of 1968 was not the first national effort to deal with the problems of firearms in

American life. In 1919, Congress had voted for a 10 percent manufacturer's tax on firearms, reasoning that taxing weapons would make them more expensive to buy. In 1927, Congress prohibited the interstate mailing of guns. Both laws were only weak attempts to regulate weapons, however, since guns could still be stolen or sent across state lines without using the United States mail.

In 1934, hoping to cut off the supply of readily available machine guns to gangs of hoodlums, Congress passed the National Firearms Act. This law made it a requirement that the following rules be observed:

1. Owners of machine guns, sawed-off shotguns or sawed-off rifles had to register them with the federal government within 60 days.

2. Manufacturers of all guns were required to use serial numbers on them (to make keeping track of individual weapons possible).

3. Gun dealers, importers, and manufacturers (of the so-called "gangster weapons") had to be licensed.

The Federal Firearms Act of 1938 subjected firearms to further regulations:

1. Sellers of guns had to pay taxes on them.

2. Dealers had to keep accurate records of firearms sales; that is, who they were sold to.

3. Certain persons (such as convicted felons) could not buy guns.

4. Only federally-licensed dealers could ship guns across state lines.

For the most part, the Gun Control Act of 1968 was simply an effort to make these existing federal laws more specific and restrictive, but it added a few new restrictions as well. For example, it prohibited the importing of all military weapons except those used for sports and hunting. And perhaps, most significantly, it made illegal the importing of cheap handguns—those "Saturday night specials."

To some extent, this law was not very realistic. After all, it could only deal with a few specific gun types sold to Americans after 1968. Banning imported cheap hanguns did not stop domestic manufacturers from continuing to produce them. Also, millions of Americans already owned guns, many thousands of which are stolen every year. Although the 1968 law would accomplish very little to reduce gun violence, many people saw it as an important step whose time had come.

This law also had many other weaknesses. It allowed dealers to rely on a gun buyer's word that he or she lived in the state where they were buying the gun. It regulated sales between dealers and customers only, and did nothing about sales between private parties. And cheap, imported guns could still be sold in unassembled kit form.

In a nation with so many privately owned guns, the Gun Control Act of 1968 could hardly hope to slow the national death rate resulting from gunshots. And it did not prevent further attempts—some successful, some not—on the lives of public figures. Former Alabama Governor George Wallace was paralyzed by a gun attack during the 1972 presidential campaign. In 1975, two attempts—using handguns—were made on the life of then-President Gerald Ford. In 1980, former Beatle John Lennon was shot and killed in New York.

Civil rights leader Martin Luther King, Jr.—whom Americans now honor with a national holiday—was slain by a gunman in 1968. The killing sparked rioting throughout the United States for several days and nights.

Each time a gun tragedy occurred, many Americans raised their voices and wrote to their congressmen demanding gun control action. But gun control opponents have been tough lobbyists, and gun control remained a lost cause.

Then, on March 31, 1981, President Ronald Reagan and his press secretary, James Brady, were shot and wounded in Washington, D.C. Brady nearly died from his wound, and is permanently paralyzed. President Reagan was luckier. After being released from the hospital after a short stay, he continued for seven years as president. A lifelong member of the National Rifle Association (or NRA, a pro-gun lobby), Reagan still insisted that the federal government stay out of gun regulation. On the other hand, James Brady and his wife Sarah have become staunch anti-gun activists.

Meanwhile, those who believed that the 1968 Gun Control Act was wrong began lobbying to get rid of it. Chief among these groups was the National Rifle Association.

FOUR

"GUNS DON'T KILL PEOPLE"

The National Rifle Association was formed in 1871 by a group of war veterans who wanted to keep the quality of American gun skills high. At first, the NRA was largely a club for gun enthusiasts, people who enjoyed well-made or antique guns, excellent marksmanship, and hunting for wild game.

In the late 1970s, the NRA experienced a conflict. The older members wanted to leave Washington, D.C. and become more of a gun club for gun hobbyists and less of a political force. But this group was outnumbered by younger NRA members, who didn't like the idea of the federal government restricting gun ownership. When the younger group got its wish, the NRA became stronger than ever before. It recruited many new members, and it stepped up its efforts to influence Congress.

Special interest groups like the NRA hire persuasive men and women known as lobbyists. Lobbyists establish personal contact with politicians and then "help" them understand complex issues by representing the views of their own special interest group as being the most correct. While some lobbying groups do serve a strictly educational purpose, many serve only the special interests of the groups who hire, train and pay their salaries.

NRA lobbyists seek to persuade Congress that the NRA's ideas about guns are both practical and valuable. The NRA always makes sure that politicians understand that NRA members will vote for officials who support NRA ideas.

What does the NRA believe about gun control legislation? Briefly, it interprets the Second Amendment as meaning that every American has the right to manufac-

This teenager is competing with adults in a trap shooting contest. Shooting at moving targets is just one of many skill sports associated with guns, which are very popular throughout the United States.

ture, transport, buy and sell guns without any interference whatsoever from the federal government.

Today the NRA has about 2.8 million dues-paying members. There are also many people who don't belong to the association who will vote for politicians who share the NRA's philosophy. The NRA publishes five gun-related magazines that always contain articles explaining NRA beliefs about gun control. Sales from advertising help pay for many of the NRA's lobbying activities.

To advance its views about gun control, publish its magazines, and administer a few gun-safety programs, the NRA employs a staff of 365 workers, 30 of whom work as lobbyists. In 1989 alone, the NRA spent about $21 million opposing various efforts to pass laws regulating guns. The association has also contributed more than $3 million to the political campaigns of officials whose beliefs are similar to those held by the NRA.

This intense lobbying of public officials at both state and national levels is not uncommon among many groups who take a strong position on pubic policy. It is both legal and the right of everyone in a democratic system to join such groups. Voters band together precisely so they will have more political muscle to get their way.

Public Relations And Gun Policy

As a part of its continuing efforts to influence public opinon, the NRA also pays for advertising—some of which makes use of celebrities. One example is Hollywood actor Charlton Heston, well-known to most Americans for his role as Moses in the movie *The Ten Commandments*. These days he is a spokesman for the National Rifle Association.

In a recent television ad, Heston stood on a street in Washington, D.C. While sirens blared in the background, Heston spoke about the city's high murder rate and strict gun laws. His message and the NRA's message was clear: if Washington's murder rate is high despite strict gun control laws, then gun control

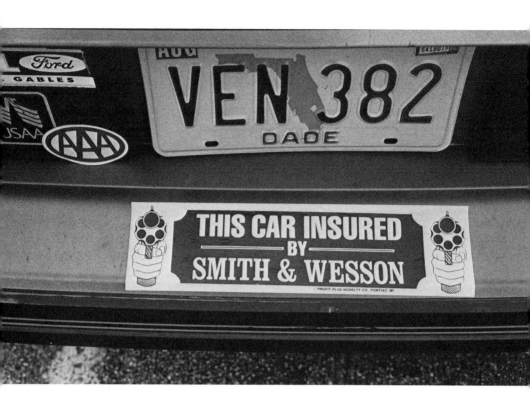

A bumper sticker on this Florida car tells everyone that the owner probably opposes any form of gun control ("Smith & Wesson" is a gun manufacturer). People against gun control firmly believe that any laws restricting their "right to bear arms" is in direct violation of the Second Amendment to the Constitution.

laws must be worthless. Not only that, they disarm law-abiding citizens who have a right to defend themselves against criminals.

But this was not the whole story. Washington, D.C. not only has a major drug problem, but it is an isolated district surrounded by several states where buying guns is easy. This is especially true of Virginia, where a gun can be bought over the counter with just a driver's license and cash. Many of the murders mentioned in the NRA ad were undoubtedly committed with guns bought in Virginia. And many of the guns used in the killings were probably purchased before the city implemented its strict laws. And certainly many of the weapons used had been stolen.

Since guns do not wear out quickly and can be used for many years, the effect of any legislation will always be limited. That is why gun control advocates say that if guns can be easily bought in Virginia and used a short time later to kill in Washington, D.C., gun control efforts have to be nationwide to be effective. And it would take years before the effect of any gun law restrictions would be felt in the community. Older guns would eventually fall into disuse, and more guns confiscated by the police during crimes.

National Rifle Association members, however, believe that guns have been a force for good. They say that government by moderation and compromise has worked in America only because of widespread gun ownership. They insist that even our enemies have preferred to negotiate rather than fight with armed American citizens.

Gun owners also possess guns for more reasons that just self-defense. Target shooting is a popular sport, and there are even target shooting events in both the summer and winter Olympic Games. Hunting game may be a controversial activity to some people, but it is still widely practiced in many states.

Hunting is regulated by the states; only certain species of wildlife may be hunted for a limited time in specific regions. Although animal rights activists argue that all hunting is morally wrong, even wildlife conservationists recommend certain types of "hunts" to help control game populations that might overrun certain habitats. These habitats can be ruined for other species. Whether hunting is an ecological need or a human urge, the debate over using guns to kill animals is not likely to be resolved any time soon.

"People Kill People"

To the NRA, the high rate of gun deaths in America should be blamed on the people who own guns, not the guns themselves. Their favorite slogan is, "Guns don't kill people. People kill people." The NRA favors longer prison sentences for Americans who commit crimes with guns, not taking guns away from law-abiding citizens. Unfortunately, long prison sentences won't save the lives that have already been claimed by gunshots. And the "guns don't kill people" argument can be disputed.

For example, an eight-year-old boy in Fairfax, Virginia, accidentally shot his six-year-old sister to death by just picking up a handgun that had fallen on the floor. In Creswell, Oregon, a pistol fell from a closet shelf and discharged, shooting a young boy in the stomach. So-called freak accidents like these are bound to happen in a country with more than 50 million guns. In other words, guns don't have to be pointed at someone in anger in order to be deadly.

In response to these accidents, the NRA says that they are the result of gun owners who are poorly trained in the handling of firearms. They believe that poor supervision in the home and the failure to lock up loaded guns are the problems, not the guns.

An objection to the "guns don't kill people" theory has been raised by Robert Lawrence, a pathologist whose job it is to study dead people's corpses to determine how they died. He tells about the case of a man

A gun instructor (left) trains a pupil at a pistol shooting range in Cincinnati, Ohio. Many more women are buying and learning to use guns for protection.

beaten to death with a car jack.

"If you hit somebody enough times with a blunt object to kill them, you probably mean to kill them," he says. "That is not, in my opinion, always true with a firearm case. There are plenty of cases that involve a spur-of-the-moment lapse of judgment or an intense moment of irresponsibility under the influence of alcohol or drugs, when a person will shoot somebody before that person realizes what they're doing. And once that weapon discharges, it's all over. It's too late. Once they pull a trigger their options are gone."

Guns, in other words, are very efficient for killing.

The fact is that not everyone has the strength and skill required to beat another person to death with a heavy instrument. Confronted by someone wielding a knife or club, many people have managed to fight back and save themselves. It is much harder to run away from a bullet. Old people, little people, cowardly people: a gun can make a killer out of people who otherwise would not have the strength or the sustained anger to kill.

Put another way, gun control advocates believe that while crime may not be reduced overall by having stricter gun laws, the amount of death certainly can be.

FIVE

CONTROL VERSUS DECONTROL

With the passage of the 1968 Gun Control Act, the NRA went on the offensive to have the act revoked or at least amended to remove some of its restrictions. The eventual result was the sponsorship of the McClure-Volkmer Gun Decontrol bill.

Shortly before the McClure-Volkmer bill was introduced to the Senate, the NRA contributed $95,000 to the 1983-1984 political campaigns of several senators known to be sympathetic to NRA views on gun control. The intent of the bill was to undo many of the restrictions imposed by the 1968 Gun Control Act. After the NRA-supported politicians were elected to the Senate, the McClure-Volkmer bill came before the Senate and passed easily.

The House of Representatives finally voted an amended McClure-Volkmer bill into law in April of 1986. Accordingly, the 1968 Gun Control Act was weakened. Handguns and rifles can now be legally transported across state borders—just as Patrick Edward Purdy transported his AK-47 from Oregon to California. Gun dealers can sell weapons from their "personal collections" without keeping records. Federal agents must meet tougher standards to prove a citizen has violated gun laws, and the law now limits federal access to a gun dealer's records. Agents must also give advance notice of an intention to inspect a gun dealer's place of business.

The Effect Of The Purdy Massacre

About three years after the McClure-Volkmer bill became law, when Patrick Purdy murdered the children

The drive by concerned citizens to ban handguns in local communities has gained strength in the past ten years. More states are passing stricter gun control laws to make it harder to buy certain types of guns.

in the Stockton schoolyard, the NRA began raising a large amount of money. It was afraid that Purdy's crime would once again arouse public feelings on the subject of gun control, and its membership worried that local governments would begin to work to ban assault rifles.

When such a movement did indeed materialize, the NRA had already raised $9 million to fight against gun control legislation. For a time it looked as if outrage over the Purdy shootings might lead to new gun control laws. The NRA had been correct: some cities and states looked for new ways to fight the availability of deadly weapons in their communities.

California led the way. Its 80-member state assembly narrowly banned the manufacture and sale of automatic weapons within the state. Before the law could be put into effect, however, many gun enthusiasts rushed out to buy assault weapons. Gun shops sold every assault weapon they had in stock—sometimes for double and triple their original prices.

Other states considered similar legislation, but faced with stiff opposition by the NRA and other gun groups, they gave up—at least for the time being.

President Bush, a lifetime NRA member, at first responded to the cry for gun legislation by saying he would not impose a federal ban on assault weapons. But many people disagreed with Bush's stand, including his wife Barbara, Los Angeles Police Chief Daryl Gates, "Drug Czar" William Bennett and Stephen Higgins, director of the Bureau of Alcohol, Tobacco and Firearms. Eventually, President Bush was persuaded to ban 43 different types of imported assault weapons, but this ban would have no effect on the more than 300,000 privately-owned assault weapons made in America. American manufacturers are free to continue producing these guns (although one company—Colt Industries—voluntarily suspended commercial sales of its AR-15, a civilian version of America's military assault rifle, the M-16).

Although the NRA has been able to raise millions of dollars quickly to combat any gun control efforts, there is some evidence that it no longer enjoys the strong support it once did. For example, despite a $6.6 million campaign conducted by the NRA against an existing law, Maryland has refused to repeal a law that banned certain handguns in that state. And, although Congress has been reluctant to consider or enact legislation aimed at dealing with the gun problem, the NRA has recently begun to lose ground to those who believe that efforts to control guns might eventually reduce gunshot deaths.

Gunning For The NRA

Recently, 140,000 Parade magazine readers responded to four gun-control proposals made by judge Warren E. Burger, once chief justice of the United States Supreme Court. He called on Americans to think about gun control. Of those responding to the survey, 67 percent said that a ten-day waiting period to purchase a gun was a reasonable requirement (29 percent disagreed). Sixty-three percent also said that a gun buyer should fill out an application that asked for age, criminal record, and other information (20 percent disagreed). Sixty-four percent believed that the transfer of ownership of a gun, like that of a car, should be officially recorded with the state (31 percent said it should not). Sixty-five percent thought every gun should be "ballistically fingerprinted"—that is, the unique marks left on every bullet fired by an individual weapon should be on file, along with information about the owner of the weapon (32 percent said no).

A recent Harris poll found that 70 percent of the country's handgun owners favored handgun registration. And yet another poll conducted by Cable News Network and Time suggested that despite NRA opposition to any waiting period for those wanting to buy a handgun, fully 87 percent of the nation's gun owners are in favor of such a "cooling-off period." (It's called a "cooling-off period" because people have been known to rush out and buy a gun when they are angry so they can kill themselves or someone else.)

The NRA argues with the results of this last poll. It also insists that 66 percent of its $77 million annual budget continues to come from the public, and that its contributions would not be so high if support for the NRA philosophy was weak. Many people believe, however, that it is the gun dealers and manufacturers who are funneling more money to the NRA than ever before.

The NRA has started to lose much of its traditional support among police because it continues to favor unrestricted sales of assault weapons at a time when many police are outgunned by street criminals. But law enforcement agencies have been even more disappointed with the NRA for its stand on the issues of Teflon bullets and plastic handguns.

Teflon Bullets

The police tend to accept the need for self-defense and the rights of citizens to protect private property. Most policemen and policewomen are good shots, and have been taught the principles of gun safety and marksmanship. Many of them enjoy hunting.

In recent years, however, police have fallen out with the NRA because of the association's attitude toward Teflon bullets. Teflon is a plastic. When it is used to coat ammunition, the result is what are known as "cop killer" bullets, so-called because they can pierce the bullet-proof protective vests often worn by law enforcement officers. At first, the NRA fought legislation to ban the bullets. But gradually, under intense and organized pressure from police and other groups, the association agreed to support a law that banned most Teflon bullets.

Plastic Handguns

Many plastics have recently become durable enough to withstand the stresses of gunpowder and bullets. A firearms manufacturer in Austria built the first plastic handguns a few years ago, and other companies have since followed suit.

Because these weapons have only a few metal parts, they can be taken apart, placed in a suitcase (for example), and deceive all but the most sensitive electronic security devices installed at airports. Guns taken aboard planes have been used in hijackings, murders, and many acts of terrorism.

Except for the fact that they are hard to detect electronically, plastic handguns are really no more powerful than other handguns. Terrorism would seem to be their only purpose. Yet, as with Teflon bullets, the NRA had to be pressured into accepting a bill to prevent the importation or manufacture of plastic handguns. This law, however, does not cover plastic handguns already purchased.

Assault Weapons

Most weapons require the manual operation of a lever or bolt to eject a spent shell before another round can be fired. But some weapons, commonly called "assault" weapons, are semiautomatics. This means they fire, eject, and automatically load another cartridge for firing—all in an instant—and with a single pull of the trigger. Although they can also be shotguns or handguns, most assault weapons are rifles. Assault weapons were developed for military use under the highly mobile conditions of modern warfare. Typically they are strongly built, lightweight, and inexpensive to manufacture.

Although the armies of most countries have had assault rifles for many years, only recently have some civilian populations had access to them. Authorities believe the weapons have become popular because of the increase in international drug dealing and because they have been glamorized in films and on television. Whereas only 4,000 Chinese-made AK-47s were sold in the United States in 1985-86, sales of that gun alone leaped to 40,000 in both 1988 and 1989. Sales of the MAC-10, an inexpensive American made semiautomatic, have also skyrocketed.

Patrick Purdy shot the Stockton school children with an AK-47, a semiautomatic rifle costing less than $400. At the time he bought it, such a weapon could have been purchased in almost any city or state. Similar weapons made by American manufacturers can still be bought in any state except California.

Automatic weapons continue to fire as long as the user keeps the trigger depressed, and as long as the weapon has access to fresh ammunition. Such fully automatic weapons must be registered with local and federal authorities. Sales must be accompanied by fingerprints, certification by a law enforcement agency, and payment of a $200 tax. Not everyone is qualified to buy or willing to go to so much trouble to own one of these guns, but it is not really necessary. With a little know-how, semiautomatic assault weapons can be turned into machine guns—some very easily.

Federal Drug Enforcement Agency officers have recently begun to carry automatic weapons. They are afraid of being outgunned by drug dealers with automatic and semiautomatic weapons. On the local level, many police departments and officers have begun switching from service revolvers to semiautomatic handguns.

Unfortunately, when a policeman armed with only an eight-shot pistol is confronted by someone armed with a semiautomatic rifle with a 75-shot clip, the policeman is going to be outgunned. Not surprisingly, more and more law enforcement officers have come out in favor of banning sales of assault weapons. They cannot understand why the NRA continues to advocate sales of weapons that authorities say have no true sporting use.

SIX

DRUGS AND GUNS

Of the 464 gun-shot deaths cataloged in one week by *Time* magazine, at least 60 were linked to drug and alcohol abuse. Others—particularly those of young men shot on the streets by apparent strangers—suggest probable connections with illegal drug activity. Police know that drug users in search of money commit many burglaries and robberies. Because many fatal shootings occur during drug-related crimes, drugs and guns directly influence the death rate. Many of the more than 200 suicides in the survey were committed by young people, those most inclined to abuse drugs.

Drugs and guns go together like salt and pepper. In Southern California, gangs selling drugs often shoot members of rival gangs who are engaged in the same activity. In search of revenge, angry gang members will often pile into a car, cruise the streets, and look for someone to punish. If they can't find the person who shot one of their own, they will target one of his "homeboys"—a friend, a family member or neighbor. There are hundreds of such shootings every year.

Not long ago a nationally famous newspaper columnist, Mary McGrory, criticized President Bush for giving a 23-minute anti-drug talk on television without ever mentioning guns. McGrory pointed out that drug dealers are almost always armed with powerful weapons, and that she doubted Bush could persuade people he was serious about the "war on drugs" without also acknowledging the need for some kind of a war on weapons.

International Consequences

United States gun sales also affect other countries.

Guns And Murders

The gun continued to be the leader in murder weapons throughout the 1980s, as shown in the chart below. Stabbing remains a distant second.

Year	Murder Victims [Total]	By Guns	Percent
1980	21,860	13,650	62.0
1981	20,053	12,523	62.4
1982	19,485	11,721	60.2
1983	18,673	10,895	58.0
1984	16,689	9,819	58.8
1985	17,545	10,296	58.7
1986	19,257	11,381	59.1
1987	17,859	10,556	59.1
1988	18,269	11,084	60.7

Source: Department of Justice, Federal Bureau of Investigation, Uniform Crime Reports for the United States, 1989.

Drug dealers from South America, Asia and other parts of the world regularly send representatives here to buy guns in states that have easy gun laws. One such "gun broker" was recently arrested in Italy. Italian customs officials knew him well, and he had recently been arrested in California for trying to smuggle ten American-made assault rifles out of the country.

Colombia is the South American country most widely blamed for processing and smuggling cocaine that shows up in America's illegal drug market. But Colombian President Virgilio Barco recently argued that the American government has not been doing its part in the war on drugs. More than he blames the government, however, Barco blames American firearms manufacturers and dealers for many of the drug problems in Colombia. Why? American-made semiautomatic assault rifles smuggled into Colombia are used regularly to kill local judges, senators, mayors and politicians in an effort to halt that country's efforts to crack down on drugs. Americans want the supply of Colombian-processed cocaine to stay out of the United States, and Barco wants to keep American-made assault weapons out of Colombia.

When the U.S. Bureau of Alcohol, Tobacco and Firearms recently studied 158 guns taken by police from drug criminals in Colombia, 85 came from Florida. Eighty percent of the guns were stamped, "Made in America."

While conservatives say they want to get tough on crime, and the NRA supports the building of more jail cells, both groups still continue to demand easy access to weapons that help make the crime rate grow. Gun control proponents say it is a waste of time to want tough criminal penalties for those who use guns to commit crimes, while doing nothing to prevent or make it harder for criminals to get guns. Can one hate killing, yet love the instruments used to kill?

Is Compromise Possible?

While the NRA and other gun enthusiasts insist on emphasizing the second half of the Second Amendment ("the right of the people to keep and bear arms shall not be infringed"), gun control advocates call attention to the first half ("A well-regulated militia being necessary to the security of a free state...").

Opponents of gun control insist that the right of a citizen to keep and bear arms cannot be changed without violating the Second Amendment of the Constitution. They point out that history has smiled on people who were strong and willing to resist tyranny. They maintain that the police are not always able to provide the protection needed by American citizens, and that a gun wielded in self-defense can be an equalizer between a law-abiding citizen and a drug-crazed psychopath. There is something in the NRA argument that appeals to a deeply seated human need to retain control over our own lives. Although most Americans like to believe in peace, few want peace at any cost. Few want to live with the knowledge that should criminals intrude into their homes, they could not defend themselves and their loved ones.

On the other side of this controversy, gun control advocates insist that there is an obvious connection between the number of guns privately owned by Americans and the number of Americans shot and

This load of semiautomatic weapons was seized by U.S. Customs inspectors in Miami, Florida. The shipment was bound for Colombia, the South American country that produces most of the cocaine consumed in the United States.

killed. They point out that while there is nothing wrong with owning a weapon for self-defense purposes, many weapons are not properly stored, and are too often either found and used by children or stolen and used by criminals. Since guns most often kill the people who own them or people known to them, gun control advocates argue that guns are not for everyone.

Gun control advocates also want to create a system that will be able to distinguish between weapons obtained for sport and legitimate self-defense, and those bought by people like Patrick Purdy. This, needless to say, is a very difficult thing to accomplish—maybe even impossible. But since a comprehensive system for controlling the ownership of guns has never been tried in the United States, it's hard to know for certain.

A professor of constitutional law at the University of Texas believes that the gun control issue can lend itself to compromise. Sanford Levinson says that the Second Amendment must be looked at as providing guidance rather than rigidity. He thinks that the Amendment fails to offer either side of the gun control argument with the solution each seeks.

"The amendment might not permit the extent of gun control that most of us—that is, liberal academics—would like," he admits. "But the NRA argument that it permits no control at all is nonsense. Even the ACLU [the American Civil Liberties Union, an association dedicated to issues arising in connection with the Bill of Rights] admits that there are some times when you can take away people's freedom of speech. So the issue is to what extent does the Second Amendment permit the government to do what it wants in controlling firearms, just as we have to establish the extent to which it can limit speech or break into your house without a warrant." Levinson believes that Americans have to find a balance between the practical and the constitutional.

Levinson admits that the Second Amendment applies not only to state militias but to individuals. He says that at the time the Bill of Rights was written, the militia was each and every person. Taking the Bill of Rights seriously, he argues, means "that one will honor them [rights] even when there is significant social cost in doing so."

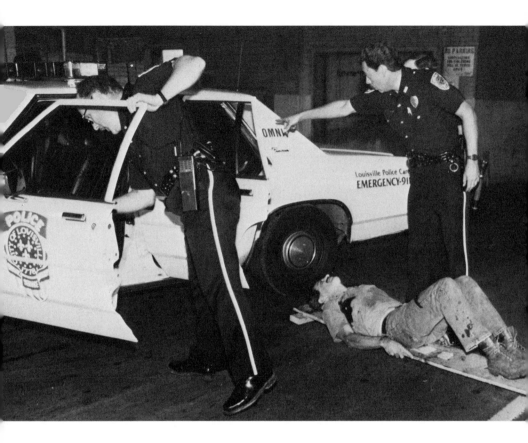

These police are helping a victim of a shooting spree in a Louisville, Kentucky, printing plant. Eight persons were killed and 12 wounded during the incident, which occurred in 1989.

Laurence H. Tribe, a professor of constitutional law at Harvard University, argues that the courts have already decided overwhelmingly against a universal right to bear arms. Even if such a law existed, says Tribe, "that would not prevent reasonable regulations from being upheld."

Perhaps the gun control issue could benefit from an extended comparison to the issues arising out of the ownership of a car. While the Constitution protects private property, federal, state, and city governments have subjected cars to a variety of controls and taxes.

Drivers are tested to be sure they know and are willing to obey the laws. Drivers are required to have reached the age of 16 to ensure a degree of maturity. Cars are inspected for safety purposes so that other drivers are not endangered needlessly. Insurance is required to protect other drivers. Gasoline and oil are taxed by governments to maintain the roads and highways and keep them safe. Drunken drivers are put in jail.

Gun control advocates feel that some regulation of deadly weapons is called for in a society with as many social frictions as ours. Gun defenders believe that any erosion in the right of Americans to own guns will lead to totalitarian threats or, at the very least, leave law-abiding citizens defenseless against criminals. But gun control is not the same as a gun ban, or complete prohibition of guns. Cars are not banned, their use is just restricted.

Do Americans have as much right to curb careless gun use as drivers and their passengers have to survive the roads and highways of America?

Glossary

ASSAULT WEAPON. Label generally given to any gun type that is manufactured with intended military purposes.

AUTOMATIC WEAPON. A weapon is "fully automatic" if it continues to fire rounds as long as the trigger is kept depressed.

CALIBER. The size of a bullet or shell as measured by its diameter; also the diameter of the gun barrel.

LOBBY. An organized citizen or business group that persuades legislators to vote pro or con on specific causes; the National Rifle Association acts as a lobby on gun control issues.

ROUND. A single shot from any weapon.

SATURDAY NIGHT SPECIAL. Slang term for an inexpensive handgun, easily concealed and not made for any sporting uses.

SECOND AMENDMENT. The amendment in the Bill of Rights that gun control opponents cite as the cornerstone of their right to gun ownership.

SEMIAUTOMATIC WEAPON. Any gun type that automatically loads another bullet into the firing position after the trigger has been pulled. Also called "self-loading." The trigger must be depressed each time to fire a round and load another.

Bibliography

Flynn, George and Alan Gottlieb. *Guns for Women: The Complete Handgun Buying Guide for Women*. Merril Press, Bellvue, Washington, 1988

Gardner, Ann and Michael Clancy. *Firearms Statutes in the United States*. United States Conference of Mayors

Hogg, Ian V. and John Weeks. *Military Small Arms of the 20th Century*. DBI Books, Northbrook, IL, 1985

Lambert, Richard B., Editor, Alan W. Heston, Assistant Editor. *The Annals of the American Academy of Political and Social Science: GUN CONTROL*. Philadelphia, 1981

Warner, Ken, Editor. *Gun Digest* 1987 41st Annual Edition, DBI Books, Inc., Northbrook, IL, 1986

Wright, James D. and Peter H. Rossi. *Armed and Considered Dangerous: A Survey of Felons and Their Firearms*. Aldine de Gruyter, Hawthorne, NY 1986

Wright, James D., Peter H. Rossi, and Kathleen Daly. *Under the Gun: Weapons, Crime, and Violence in America*. Aldine Publishing Company, Hawthorne, NY, 1983

Index

Picture Credits